THREE STARS IN THE NIGHT SKY

Other books by Fern Schumer Chapman

NON-FICTION
Brothers, Sisters, Strangers:
Sibling Estrangement and the Road to Reconciliation

MEMOIR
Motherland:
A Mother/Daughter Journey to Reclaim the Past

YOUNG ADULT HISTORICAL FICTION
Is It Night or Day?

YOUNG ADULT NON-FICTION
Facing the Past:
A Public Memorial Compels a Small
German Town to Confront Its History

Middle School Sleuths:
How an Eighth-Grade Class Reunited Two
Holocaust Refugees

CHILDREN'S PICTURE BOOKS
Happy Harper Thursdays:
A Grandmother's Love for Her Granddaughter
during the Coronavirus

The Return of Happy Harper Thursdays:
The Guiding Light of a Grandmother's Love

For more information, please visit:
www.fernschumerchapman.com

THREE STARS IN THE NIGHT SKY

A Holocaust Family's Odyssey of Separation and Reunion

FERN SCHUMER CHAPMAN

GUSSIE ROSE PRESS

Published October 25, 2023, by Gussie Rose Press, Lake Bluff, Illinois

Book cover design by Sean Michael Severino and interior design by Tom Greensfelder

ISBN numbers:

Publisher's Cataloging-in-Publication data

Names: Chapman, Fern Schumer, author.

Title: Three stars in the night sky : a Holocaust family's odyssey of separation and reunion / Fern Schumer Chapman.

Series: The Legacy of the Holocaust

Description: Lake Bluff, IL: Gussie Rose Press, 2023. | Summary: At just 12, Gerda Katz braved the journey from Nazi Germany to America all by herself as an unaccompanied minor. Her family escaped to the Dominican Republic — one of there few countries that offers Jews a haven during the Holocaust. Separated for 21 years, Gerda's experiences spotlight her profound loneliness as she adjusts to a new language, culture, and country without her family.

Identifiers: LCCN: 2023920186 | ISBN: 978-1-962817-04-2 (hardcover) | 979-8-9872597-7-1 (paperback) | 978-1-962817-05-9 (ebook)

Subjects: Katz, Gerda--Juvenile literature. | Jewish children in the Holocaust--Juvenile literature. | Refugee children--Biography--Juvenile literature. | Jewish refugees--United States--History--Juvenile literature. | Jewish refugees--Dominican Republic—History--Juvenile literature. | BISAC JUVENILE NONFICTION / History / Holocaust | JUVENILE NONFICTION / Social Topics / Prejudice & Racism

Classification: LCC D804.3 .C43 2023 | DDC 940.53/18--dc23

For Ann Sherman

And for all child refugees forced to leave
their homelands and families

"...UND WENN SIE NICHT GESTORBEN SIND, DANN LEBEN SIE NOCH HEUTE."

"...AND IF THEY ARE NOT DEAD, THEN THEY ARE STILL ALIVE TODAY."

—THE ENDING OF MANY GRIMMS' FAIRY TALES

Children have been coming alone to America for hundreds of years.

Today, unaccompanied minors are part of the greatest surge of migration since World War II. In recent years, nearly 150,000 children travelling all by themselves have come to our borders annually — some as young as 7 years old. Most are fleeing wars and conflicts in Central and South America, the Middle East, and Africa. These forced refugees undertake their journeys for many reasons: war, famine, political persecution, gang warfare and corruption, crushing poverty, natural disasters. Some are escaping violence; some want to reunite with family; some are seeking a better life.

The routes these children take are often unimaginably dangerous. These children are vulnerable to human trafficking, forced labor, and slavery. Many countries can't keep up with the surge of migrants; consequently, some unaccompanied minors end up in shelters or living on the streets of their new country. Even those who find a home struggle to learn a different language and culture, and to establish a life without their families in a new land.

Throughout history, the United States has seen several waves of child immigration. For example:

- During the Potato Famine of the late 1840s, Irish parents who couldn't afford to feed their children sent them on ships to the U.S. The sad partings at the docks were called "American wakes."

- British families sent 5,000 of their children to safety in the U.S. during the World War II German blitz of England.

- More than 27,000 child refugees fleeing the murderous Sudanese civil war have come to America.

- Parents in Mexico and Central and South America, who desperately want their children to have a better education and a safer life, continue to send their sons and daughters to live in this country.

Unaccompanied minors in history: Jewish refugee children flee Nazi-occupied Austria in 1939.

Each child refugee has his or her own dramatic story. Yet, all unaccompanied minors share common experiences — loss of homeland, language, identity, and family. These emotional uprootings often cast these young people adrift, even when they've escaped great harm.

One young Jewish refugee during World War II, Gerda Katz, was only twelve years old when her family, fearful of growing anti-Jewish hatred, secured a spot on a ship from Nazi Germany to America. She was fortunate to have a place to go, as a Jewish family offered young Gerda a room in its boarding house in Seattle, Washington.

Gerda traveled alone, with the great hope that one day she would be reunited with her parents, sister, and two brothers. But that reunion was never guaranteed. Gerda's dramatic experiences illuminate the trials, setbacks, and triumphs unaccompanied minors have faced throughout history. Gerda's story of her family's plight also highlights a little-known American rescue program.

Syrian children stand at a fence at a refugee camp near Gaziantep, Turkey.

I knew Gerda's story because she and my mother met on the *Deutschland*, the ship that brought them to America. Both traveling alone, both traumatized by the sudden changes in their lives, the girls immediately became best friends. Sadly, however, the girls lost touch soon after arriving in 1938.

Seven decades later, when a middle-school class read my historical novel, *Is It Night or Day?*, describing the girls' friendship, the students were so moved by the story that they made it a class project to reunite the pair. Fulfilling a shared lifelong dream, the two women, who were in their 80s, finally saw each other again in 2011. I have captured this remarkable reunion in my book, *Like Finding My Twin: How an Eighth-Grade Class Reunited Two Holocaust Refugees*. At that time, Gerda shared her untold story with me. Struck by her remarkable memory and artifacts — letters, documents, and photographs — I recognized the unique and universal value of her experiences.

GERDA'S CHILDHOOD IN GERMANY

For more than a millennium — 1,000 years — Gerda Katz's family lived in a quiet German town called Münzenberg, amid farms, rolling hills, and woods. This small, quaint town is best known for the Brothers Grimm, who based their famed collection of fairy tales — including "The Pied Piper of Hamelin," "Sleeping Beauty," and "Hansel and Gretel" — on ancient folklore from the region. The stories had been handed down from generation to generation in an oral tradition.

Recognizing their rich cultural value, Jacob and Wilhelm Grimm compiled the stories into their famous work, *Grimms' Fairy Tales*, first published in 1812. Gerda's favorite, "Snow White and the Seven Dwarfs," has similarities to her life. In that story, Snow White runs off to the woods in order to escape her murderous stepmother.

Gerda was born in Münzenberg in 1925, when the town was home to about 3,000 people. Most were farmers, except the six Jewish families who ran local businesses. The Katzes, an Orthodox Jewish family, owned a pharmacy that also sold shoes Gerda's mother made by hand. In the 1930s, the town had a sleepy, old-world feel, with only one car driving alongside horses and carriages on cobblestoned streets. Münzenberg didn't even have running water, so residents had to go to a local pump to get water for drinking, cooking, and bathing.

Gerda vividly remembers the impressive Castle Münzenberg, just outside of town. One of the best-preserved ruined castles in Germany from the Twelfth century and a symbol of the region, it features two imposing towers, steep hills, and grassy knolls. Remarkably, Gerda's ancestors probably watched as workmen built the fortress in 1151 to protect the town. But for Gerda, a tomboy, the ruins were her playground. "I would climb to the top of the towers and roll down the steep hills," she says. "It drove my parents crazy with worry."

"I used to climb to the top of the towers and roll down the steep hill. It drove my parents crazy."

(Left) Franz Jüttner's illustration of "Snow White and the Seven Dwarfs." (Right) Castle Münzenberg, one of the best preserved ruins from the Middle Ages.

(Left) The Katzes, pictured in the backyard of their home in 1937. The family had lived in Münzenberg, Germany, for over 1,000 years. (Below) Gerda with her pet chicken, "Laura."

The Katzes saw themselves as good and loyal Germans, especially since Gerda's father had fought for the Kaiser in World War I. Her mother, a strong, resourceful woman whom Gerda called "*Mutter*" (mother in German), loved to cook, bake and work with her "golden" hands. An important member of the Jewish community, she also prepared the dead for burial — washing and dressing the body for the religious ceremony.

The family — grandmother, mother, father, two sons, and two daughters — kept kosher (a strict Jewish diet) and attended the synagogue, located in town directly behind the Lutheran church. Gerda hated Hebrew school, so she would hide to avoid going to class. Even though Gerda hardly attended Sunday school, Gerda vividly remembers the Hebrew instructor: "Herr Pfuld," she smiles. "He was old and stern. I remember everything as if it were yesterday."

The youngest, cherished child — five years younger than her sister — Gerda felt deeply loved. "They carried me around like a doll, until I was five years old," she says. "My parents did everything for me – bathed me, washed my hair." She didn't have many toys, but she played with a ball and a cornhusk doll. Gerda remembers that she adopted one of the chickens the family kept in the yard as a pet. "Laura," she says, "I called her 'Laura.' For a time, she was my best friend." One day, when the family was eating dinner, Gerda asked which chicken had met its untimely death. Her face dropped as *Mutter* quietly whispered, "Laura."

When the Nazis came to power in the early 1930s, Gerda felt like she was living in a terrifying Grimms' fairy tale. In 1933, the charismatic Nazi leader, Adolf Hitler, became

"**They carried me around like a doll... My parents did everything for me – bathed me, washed my hair.**"

(Above and below) Local Stormtroopers rally at Castle Münzenberg in 1931 in the same location where Gerda played. (Top right) 1932 poster features a German worker towering over Jews. (Bottom right) 1938 Nazi propaganda poster proclaims, "All the people say 'Yes!'"

chancellor and promised to rebuild the country, which was still in ruins after World War I. Hitler vowed to restore national pride, which he did in part by appealing to prejudice. The Nazis believed Jews were "racially inferior," and their goal was to cleanse Germany of all Jewish influence.

Some Germans didn't agree with Hitler's anti-Jewish crusade, but everyone could see the economic progress the nation was making under Hitler. Germans — including most townspeople in Münzenberg — looked the other way as Jews were persecuted. (Hitler's private doctor even hailed from Münzenberg.) As the Nazis' grip tightened, Jews in every city, town, and village in Germany began to fear for their lives.

"I was always afraid as a child," Gerda remembers. "We had bad words written on our home, and the Nazis in brown shirts would march through the town. Jewish people — even my father and two brothers — were being picked up and released. But some never came back. The young people became fanatics right away,

Nazi Stormtroopers march in the streets of Germany in 1935.

but some old people were still our friends." Many Nazis in town owed money to the Katzes, and few neighbors came to the aid of the isolated family. "If others didn't follow Nazi orders," she explains, "they thought they would get killed."

When Nazis marched and chanted at night, Gerda and her mother hid in a kind neighbor's haystack. In the morning, they left the barn, as if they had just bought milk or butter from the farmer. Gerda was so afraid of the Nazis, she wouldn't play outside. She spent hours by herself, bouncing her ball in the house.

One day when Gerda was home alone, the Nazis banged on the front door. Gerda froze. They kicked harder and louder with their heavy boots. With her heart pounding, she finally opened the door. Two Nazis barked at Gerda, demanding she give them the family's antique gun collection. "I ran and got the guns," she says, eyes flashing again with the terror of that moment. "Then, as I gave the men the guns, I thought, 'I'll get shot. The Nazis will shoot me with our own guns.'"

"I saw Nazis everywhere. I thought about throwing myself in front of the train just to get away from the terror."

At school, teachers bullied Gerda because she was Jewish. One repeatedly hit her. When her parents complained, the headmaster said, "Don't send your daughter to school here. Then she won't get hit again."

Finally, her parents enrolled her in a Jewish school, *Israelitische Kinderheilanstalt*, in Bad Nauheim. Even though she was only eight years old, Gerda took the hour-long train ride alone. Decades later, she could still rattle off the train stops: "Münzenberg … Butzbach… Bamberg…" On the train, when a Nazi sat next to her, she would try to hide in plain sight, not moving or looking at her seatmate. "I saw them everywhere," Gerda remembers. "I was so afraid, I thought about throwing myself in front of the train just to get away from the terror."

Finally, the Katzes decided they could no longer stay in their beloved homeland of 1,000 years. However, it wouldn't be easy to get out; German officials limited the

KURT MAYER AND GERDA'S JEWISH SCHOOL IN BAD NAUHEIM

For four years, Gerda attended a school called *Israelitische Kinderheil-anstalt* in Bad Nauheim. Eight months after Gerda left for America, the Nazis organized a riot called *Kristallnacht* on November 9 and 10, 1938. During those nights, Nazis destroyed and looted Jewish businesses, cemeteries, hospitals, schools, and homes. They also murdered dozens of Jewish people. The event is known as the "Night of Broken Glass" for the shattered glass from store windows that littered the streets. Nazi-organized mobs damaged Münzenberg's synagogue and burned most of the 2,800 Jewish temples in Germany on *Kristallnacht*.

Gerda's schoolmate, Kurt Mayer, an eight-year-old boarding student at the school in 1938, witnessed some of the shocking crimes that occurred that day. He would never forget what he saw:

"I was on the top floor of the boarding school in Bad Nauheim. As we were about to get up, we heard a lot of noise, and we were told to go out on the street. We packed some clothes in suitcases, but we still had our nightshirts on and no shoes. It was cold and we were marched barefoot in a line of two or three by civilians with revolvers exposed and pointing at us. Cars driving adjacent to the sidewalk accompanied us for about one mile to the police station.

"We were held in the outside yard for several hours and I developed frostbite on my toes. Our male teachers were gone. That night we learned they had been taken to concentration camps. After what seemed an eternity, we children went back to the boarding school by ourselves. When we got back, the same men who had taken us to the police station were there and herded us around the schoolyard. We watched from the perimeter as these same men gathered prayer books and the Torah, poured gasoline on them, and burned them in the center of the schoolyard. All the kids were confused and crying."

In 2006, when Kurt Mayer and students from Pacific Lutheran University in Tacoma, Washington, visited the Bad Nauheim school, the group discovered that the nursery rhyme paintings from Gerda and Kurt's school days still adorned the walls.

The group also learned that the school had changed its name in recent decades. Now, it's called the *Sophie-Scholl-Schule Wetterau* to honor Sophie Scholl, a courageous student who belonged to a resistance group known as "The White Rose." The Nazis executed Scholl in 1943 for spreading anti-government leaflets.

On the school grounds, a small memorial honors Gerda's schoolmates who were murdered during the Holocaust.

(Top) Postcard of the school in Bad Nauheim. (Bottom) Gerda's schoolmate, Kurt Mayer. (Right) Schoolchildren and others watch Nazis burn the synagogue's prayer books and Torahs on Kristallnacht, November 1938, in Mosbach.

number of people who could get the necessary papers to emigrate, and it was difficult to find a country that would admit Jewish refugees. Still, the Katzes were determined. As Gerda explains: "Our parents didn't think anyone could survive the Nazis."

In 1938, Nazis arrested Gerda's two brothers and took them to Buchenwald, a concentration camp about 238 kilometers (150 miles) away. No one heard from Gerda's oldest brother, Adolf. In Buchenwald, Nazis severely beat Gerda's other brother, nineteen-year-old Fritz. Finally, they released him. "Fritz looked so different when he got out of the camp," Gerda remembers. "He was such a strong, cultured, intellectual man. But after being picked up, he looked small and broken."

"Fritz looked so different when he got out of the camp. After being picked up, he looked small and broken."

However, Fritz's appearance betrayed his spirit; these terrible experiences convinced him he had to get his family out of Germany. He researched every possibility and followed every lead. "My brother carried the world's burden on his shoulders," Gerda remembers. "He took care of all of us."

For Gerda, he learned of a program organized by Quaker, Lutheran, and Jewish groups that brought young people, ages 4 to 16, to safety in America. The organization operated quietly, sending just ten children at a time on cruise ships, in order to avoid the attention of anti-Jewish forces in the United States. The program saved about 100 children a year between 1934 and 1945, rescuing a total of 1,400 children.

However, Fritz doubted he could secure a spot for Gerda when he recognized that the program only selected wealthy children or the sons and daughters of rabbis. He wrote a forceful letter to the program's organizers: "All children have the same value." Surprisingly, organizers wrote back, informing him of Gerda's upcoming departure date — March 8, 1938.

(Above) Gerda's 1938 passport. (Below) Gerda's mother, Jenny Katz, and her brother, Fritz Katz, in the backyard of the family home in Münzenberg in 1938.

Gerda had only two weeks to pack her bag and get her papers in order. She went to Stuttgart, a two-hour train ride, on her own, for a physical exam for her visa. A week later, she returned to pick up her visa. She recalls, "I did everything by myself."

Gerda's classmates, including her best friend, Friedel, were sad to see her go. They compiled a *Poesiealbum*, a German autograph book, to express their best wishes in words and drawings. Days before Gerda boarded the ship, Friedel and three other classmates rode their bikes from nearby towns to Gerda's house to hug her goodbye. "They probably pedaled an hour or two uphill just to see me," she remembers. Gerda's mother had baked *Zwetschgenkuchen* (a special plum torte) for their visit. "But they didn't stay long," Gerda remembers, "They had to get home before dark. I watched them ride away."

As Gerda prepared to leave, Fritz frantically searched for a way out of Germany for the rest of the family. However, Gerda's ninety-two-year-old grandmother, whom she called "*Oma*," refused to consider any program Fritz might find. "I won't survive the trip," she insisted. "We'll carry you," Gerda's mother said. But *Oma* wouldn't budge.

Gerda hated saying goodbye to her classmates. Now, she dreaded leaving *Oma* and the rest of her family. Gerda would never forget the day she boarded the ship to America — March 8, 1938: "It was gray and cold," sobbing at the memory.

The Katzes had travelled by train to the dock in Bremenhaven. There, they joined other families being ripped apart. Parents clung desperately to their children, who wore cardboard identification tags strung around their necks. Each child's tag served as a mailing label — stating name, hometown, and destination.

"They probably pedaled an hour or two uphill just to see me. But they didn't stay long. They had to get home before dark. I watched them ride away."

(Above) The classmates who rode their bicycles to Münzenberg pose with Gerda just before she fled Nazi Germany for America in 1938.

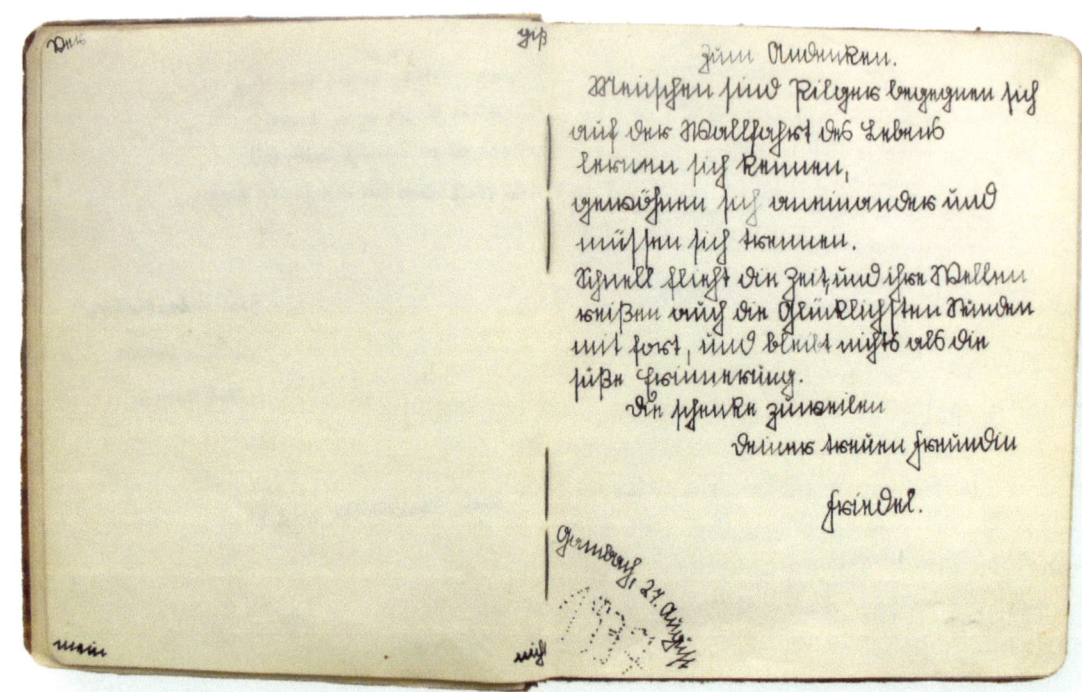

Gerda's Posiealbum, *which includes an entry from Friedel, her best friend in Germany.*

"It was so hard. I was just going through the motions. My father was crying. The parents were all crying. And we said goodbye to everyone."

On the dock, Nazis barked at Jewish families, ordering them to quickly say goodbyes "*Schnell! Schnell!*" Noticing that Gerda was crying and clinging to her cornhusk doll, one Nazi marched over, ripped the toy from Gerda's hands, and spat out, "You're too old to play with dolls!" Enraged, Gerda's father wanted to do something, but he feared he might endanger Gerda's chance at life. Instead, he reassured Gerda that she would see her family again.

"Parents were putting their children on the ship," Gerda remembers. "It was so hard. I was just going through the motions. My father was crying. The parents were all crying. And we said goodbye to everyone."

In the rush of securing papers and packing, she hadn't fully grasped what was happening to her. But, when she looked out the porthole at the rough, sea-sickening water, she realized she was leaving her home. "I saw ocean," Gerda remembers. "Then, I knew I was away."

GERDA'S NEW HOME IN SEATTLE

After ten days on the ship, three days touring New York, and six days on two trains — the *20th Century Limited* and the *Empire Builder* — taking her from New York to the West Coast, Gerda, still travelling alone with the tag around her neck, finally arrived in Seattle. To Gerda, America was as foreign as the moon. She saw things she had never encountered before: elevators, window shades, soda pop, water fountains. She was thrilled when she saw a black person for the first time on a street in New York. "*Da ist ein Afrikaner!*" she exclaimed upon the sighting. "I had only seen a black person in a picture book about Africa. So, when I saw this person, I excitedly announced, 'There is an African.'"

Skyscrapers were another surprising first for Gerda. Seattle's fourteen-story Smith Tower, built in 1914, was the tallest building west of the Mississippi River until the city built the Space Needle in 1962. A seaport city in the Pacific Northwest, Seattle, known as the Emerald City, astonished Gerda with its rolling hills and gentle rain. "I loved the beauty of the area," she remembers. "I didn't mind the rain because it made everything so lush and green in the spring." Years later, remembering her first impression of Seattle's splendor, she became an avid flower gardener, contributing in her own way to her new city's brilliance.

Gerda's new home was a small room in a large boarding house in a mixed ethnic community in east central Seattle. When Gerda first met her foster mother, Florence Flaks, a music teacher and violinist, Mrs. Flaks was wearing a fancy fur coat. "I thought she must be very rich," Gerda laughs at her memory. In reality, the Flakses were a middle-class family. Mrs. Flaks's husband, mother, aunt, and young daughter lived in the family's boarding house, along with many refugees. As president of the Seattle chapter of the National Council of Jewish Women, Mrs. Flaks sponsored Gerda, the first German refugee child in the city, in part so her

Gerda, travelling alone with the tag around her neck, finally arrived in Seattle. To Gerda, it was as foreign as the moon.

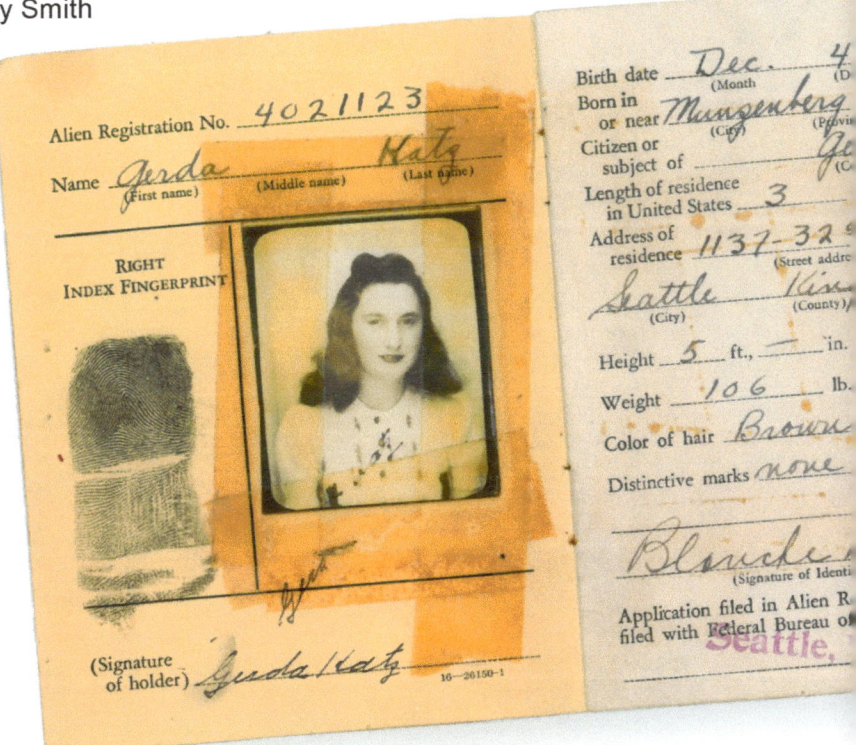

(Left) Seattle's skyline in 1938, featuring the Smith Tower, then the tallest building west of the Mississippi River. (Right) Gerda's 1941 Alien Registration card.

five-year-old daughter would have a companion. In addition, for taking care of Gerda, a Jewish immigrant aid organization paid the family $48 a month — a sizeable check during the Great Depression.

When she arrived, Gerda found a pile of letters from her family on her bed. As soon as she was alone, she opened one from her brother, Fritz: "By now you are on your way to your new home." Gerda's eyes filled with tears. "Don't be sad, my beloved sister, you will have a full life filled with laughter and joy."

On her first day at Madrona Elementary School in April of 1938, the kind principal invited her into his office. Recognizing that Gerda didn't know English, he worried she might get lost on the way to school, and she wouldn't have the words to ask for help. Every day, the principal called Gerda into his office and asked, "'Where do you live?'" she remembers. "I'd say, '1137 32nd Ave.' 'What is your phone number?' I'd say, 'PRospect 0667.'" Those were Gerda's first English words, and she would never forget her first Seattle address and phone number.

Gerda had to adjust quickly to her new residence. First, the Flaks family were Reform Jews, not Orthodox, like Gerda's family. They observed their faith in ways that were very different from the Katz family's practices. Second, she could only speak English in the Flakses' home.

The emotional adjustment was even more daunting; she had to make the transition from her loving German home, where her parents did everything for her, to the Flakses', where she had to do everything for herself.

"It was so lonely not to have my own parents. No one hugged me anymore."

"I didn't even know how to rinse out my underwear," she remembers. "I stuck my dirty undies under my mattress, until my foster mother discovered my pile and insisted I wash them out." There was little love in the boarding house. "It was so lonely not to have my own parents," Gerda remembers. "No one hugged me anymore."

In those lonely first months in Seattle, Gerda lived for the mail. Every week, her family's letters, written on international, onion-skin paper, were her greatest comfort.

(Top) Gerda's foster parents, Florence and Lewis Flaks. (Bottom) Gerda's new home, the Flakses' boarding house in Seattle.

Most started the same way, asking Gerda to thank the Flakses for their kindness in opening their home to her. The letters also revealed the family's anxieties and fears. Gerda's parents tried to advise their twelve-year-old daughter, whom they could not see, on every conceivable catastrophe:

> *Dear Gerda:*
>
> *Don't go up to dogs. Don't let dogs kiss you.*
>
> *Don't talk to strangers.*
>
> *Make sure you continue your education.*
>
> *Stay out of the sun.*
>
> *Stay away from temptations!!!*

Most of the letters ended with the same prayer: "May the Good Lord bless you and keep you safe."

When Gerda wrote back, she never told them any bad news. "I didn't want them to worry. They had so many troubles."

Every day Gerda ran to the mailbox, in hopes of hearing from her family. She kept their treasured letters in a safe place, re-reading them often and crying.

But suddenly, in 1941, the letters stopped.

Whenever Gerda opened the lid of the mailbox, barely able to breathe, she reached in with great hope. And every day she walked away, empty-handed and disappointed. The mail, which once offered comfort, now produced dread. She couldn't sleep at night, wondering and worrying about her family. "I couldn't stop thinking about them," she says.

One week turned into two. Then three.

Gerda became more agitated. "Terrible thoughts about my family haunted me. I couldn't think about anything else."

Four weeks. Five.

By now, Gerda was beside herself, not eating or sleeping, crying all the time.

Nineteen-year-old Fritz Katz, Gerda's older brother, masterminded how his family could escape Nazi Germany.

Then, one day, Gerda opened the mailbox and found an envelope addressed in Fritz's handwriting.

"I thought they had been killed," she says.

Then, one day, Gerda opened the mailbox and found an envelope addressed in Fritz's handwriting. But strangely, it didn't have the familiar German stamp with Hitler's terrifying face and Nazi insignia. Instead, a brightly colored stamp from an unknown country was pasted in the corner. She ripped open the letter, her heart pounding.

> *Sosúa, Oct. 30, 1941*
>
> *My dear sister, Gerda:*
>
> *You might be angry because you haven't heard from me. I'll surprise you with the best news. I have managed to wrest our dear parents, sister, and several relatives from Hell itself. We arrived by way of Lisbon in the Dominican Republic. The battle we faced was difficult, but God helped us. We have been saved!*
>
> *I'm sorry we couldn't save Adolf. As you know, Oma wouldn't leave; she is in a Jewish nursing home in Bad Nauheim.*
>
> *But we got out at a time when no one thought it possible for German Jews to emigrate. I never gave up hope, and I've been richly rewarded.*
>
> *Dear Gerda, maybe you can visit us one day. Please write soon, and soon you will get another letter from us.*
>
> *Many greetings and love from our parents.*
>
> *Your loving brother,*
>
> *Fritz*

The next day, Gerda brought Fritz's envelope with the bright stamp to her junior-high school. "Where is the Dominican Republic?" she asked her teachers.

No one could tell her.

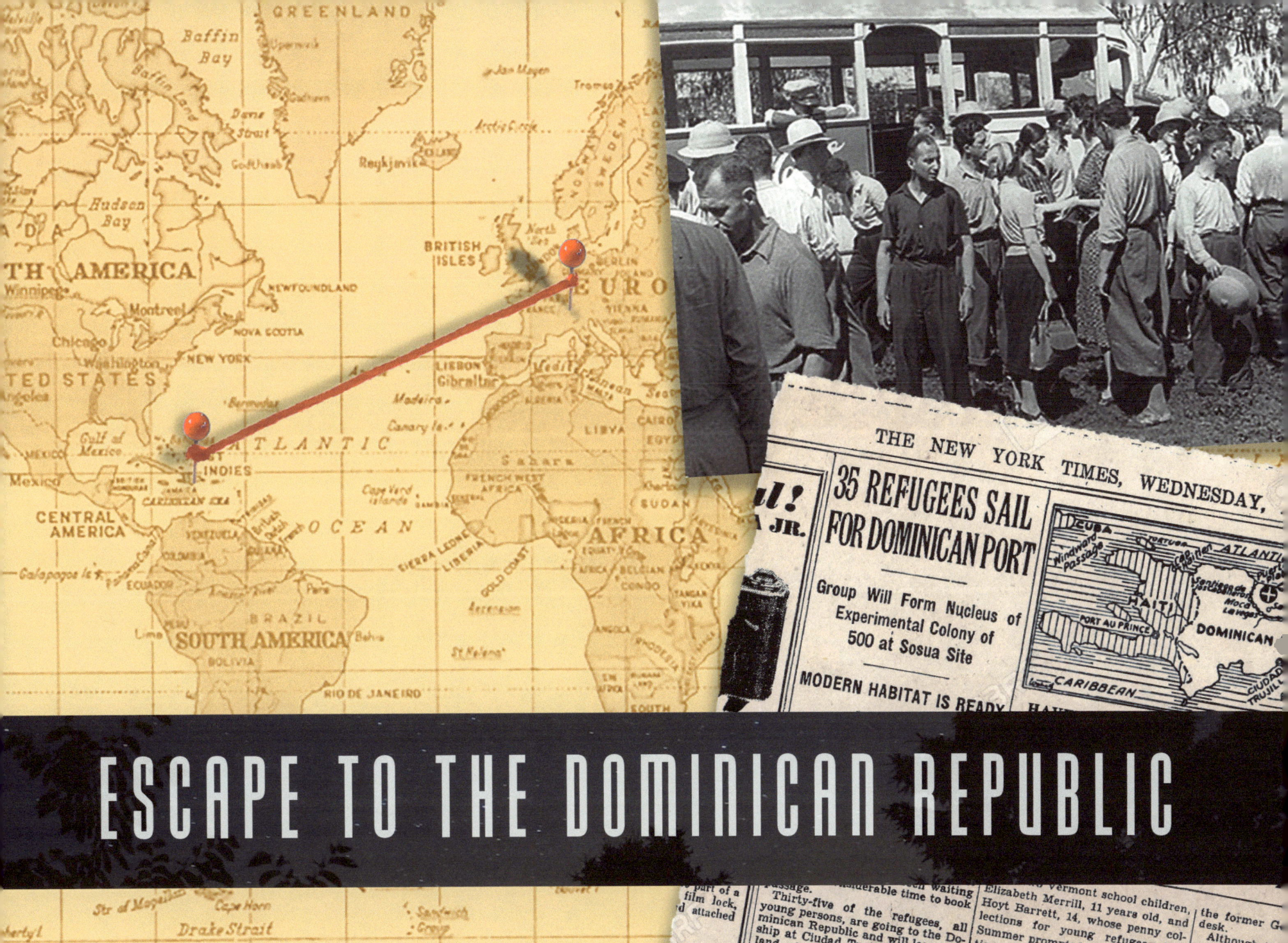

THE NEW YORK TIMES, WEDNESDAY,

35 REFUGEES SAIL FOR DOMINICAN PORT

Group Will Form Nucleus of Experimental Colony of 500 at Sosua Site

MODERN HABITAT IS READY

ESCAPE TO THE DOMINICAN REPUBLIC

Thirty-five of the refugees, all young persons, are going to the Dominican Republic and will leave the ship at Ciudad Trujillo. Others will land at ports en route, including Las Palmas, Canary Islands, and Panama.

Refugee Settlement Described

The writer of the following article has just returned from the Dominican Republic, where he investigated the small

Vermont school children. Elizabeth Merrill, 11 years old, and Hoyt Barrett, 14, whose penny collections for young refugees last Summer prompted the idea of a nation-wide Children's Crusade for Children, viewed this city as "a wonderland" yesterday under the direction of leaders of that organization.

The great contrast with their surroundings in the small community

the former G desk.

Although the gage in conversation they were intention of trophies showed them, replica of a f schooner, which to be seen along viewed the city fre leaving Mr.

erda's family escaped just weeks before the Nazis rounded up all the Jews in Münzenberg and took them to concentration camps. What saved the Katzes was a program organized by the Dominican Republic's brutal dictator, Rafael Trujillo, who ruthlessly ruled his country from 1930 to 1961.

The Dominican Republic is located on the Caribbean island of Hispaniola, which it shares with Haiti. A former colony of both Spain and France, Haiti was a French-speaking nation whose people were mostly poor, mixed-race descendants of African slaves. Trujillo always feared Haiti might try to take over his country, and, in 1937, he ordered the massacre of thousands of dark-skinned Haitians.

The world objected to this slaughter. In 1938, Trujillo attended the Evian Conference in France, where countries discussed the burgeoning Jewish refugee problem. To improve his global image and gain favor with the United States, the economic giant in the hemisphere that organized the conference, Trujillo offered to admit 100,000 Jews.

Trujillo had his own motives for welcoming Jews into his country. The dictator, who used talcum powder daily to lighten his own mixed-race complexion, wanted young European men to marry native women and produce light-skinned offspring, thereby "whitening" the Dominican people.

The European Jews, who fled a dictatorship rooted in anti-Jewish hatred, now found themselves settling in a country whose racist dictator prized their skin color over that of his own people.

Between 1940 and 1945, Trujillo issued 5,000 Dominican visas and saved about 3,000 Jews, though only 645, including Gerda's family,

(Left) The Katzes in the dining room of their small Dominican Republic homestead.
(Right) Nazi soldiers round up Jews in Budapest, October 1944.

Dominican Republic Dictator Rafael Trujillo, who used talcum powder daily to lighten his complexion.

Jews now found themselves settling in a country whose racist dictator prized their skin color over that of his own people.

settled in his country. Trujillo's government placed Jews in the remote village of Sosúa, then little more than overgrown jungle. Jews who had been professionals or craftsmen in Germany or Austria became unlikely farmers in the Dominican Republic. Each family received ten cows, a mule, a horse, and eighty acres of land in the tiny seacoast town.

In Sosúa, the transplanted German and Austrian Jews would learn to cultivate land, raise animals, establish dairy and meat industries, and build a community on an abandoned banana plantation.

The Germans who settled in the Dominican Republic were not used to the harsh, tropical climate — the burning sun, driving rain, relentless mosquitoes, threat of malaria. Residents had no hot water, no electricity, and no refrigeration. The new farmers used horses and donkeys to get around, and they had a few old tractors to work the soil. But they were delighted to rediscover fruits and vegetables that weren't available in Germany, and they even tasted fruits they had never seen before. "My sister, Edith, ate ten bananas a day when she first arrived in the DR," Gerda remembers. "She loved them."

Fritz wrote to Gerda shortly after the family arrived:

> For two months, we have been living with nine others in our own collective settlement. The conditions are poor and the mosquitoes are terrible, but we can hear the waves every day. We have farm animals and several acres of land to manage.
>
> There is no shortage of work. For now, we have a good livelihood, and, in this country, all agricultural products are available. If you're strong, there's much to do as a farmer. The work is hard, and I'm not sure we are suited to it. So we are trying to find other ways to make a living. I do administrative tasks for the settlement, and I have saved some money. You don't need to send money since I have more than you.
>
> Here, we can easily await the outcome of the war, which will decide our fate. Please don't worry. I will do everything in my power for our dear parents.

THE EVIAN CONFERENCE

Life was difficult for the 350,000 remaining Jews in Germany in the late 1930s; most were desperate to find a new place to call home. Few countries would accept Jews. Fearing they would take away jobs and burden social programs for the needy, Congress limited how many Jews could come to the United States.

Under political pressure to do something about the growing international refugee crisis, President Franklin Delano Roosevelt organized a conference at a resort in Evian, France. In the summer of 1938, delegates from thirty-two countries met to address the problem.

When Hitler learned of the Evian Conference, he gleefully commented, "I can only hope and expect that the other world, which has such deep sympathy for these criminals [Jews], will at least be generous enough to convert this sympathy into practical aid. We, on our part, are ready to put all these criminals at the disposal of these countries, for all I care, even on luxury ships."

During the nine-day meeting at Evian, country after country offered reasons why their nations could not welcome refugees:

(Bottom) The United States representative to the Evian Conference signs the agreement with the Dominican Republic to accept Jewish refugees.

- China, New Zealand, and most South American countries would not accept Jews because they claimed the Great Depression had crippled their economies.

- Australia: "We have no real racial problem, and we are not desirous of importing one."

- The British Commonwealth: "We are already overcrowded and, in any event, the climate is too severe, and, Britain is completely out of the question as a place for refugees because of the high rate of unemployment."

- France, Belgium, and the Netherlands: "We are at the extreme point of saturation in regards to admission of refugees."

- Brazil: "We are a Catholic country."

- Canada: "None is too many."

The Jewish state of Israel did not exist at that time, and most countries harbored Jewish hatred. The Dominican Republic, one of the only countries at the conference that agreed to take some Jews, would alter the course of history for the Katz family. But, for the most part, at Evian, the world quietly but firmly slammed its doors to Jewish refugees.

FRITZ WITH HORSES

THE SETTLEMENT

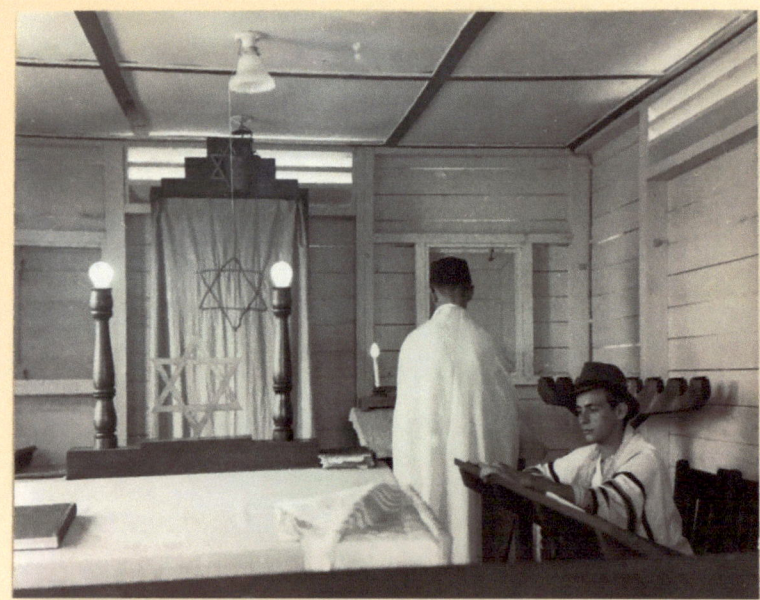

THE SYNAGOGUE

FRITZ ON THE TRACTOR

ALBERT, EDITH, & JENNY KATZ

SOSÚA SETTLEMENT

Fritz learned to drive tractors, ride horses, and till the soil; in fact, he worked so hard that he became known in the settlement as "the human tractor."

Still, it wasn't long before the settlers decided that farm life was not for them. They wanted to create a business, but they needed to produce something that didn't require electricity or refrigeration.

Their solution: "We make a very good Hollander cheese," Fritz wrote, "and I know how to make it perfectly." Jewish settlers established *Productos Sosúa*, a cooperative that marketed and sold milk and meat products from their farms. In addition, Gerda's family established a general store like the business the family had owned back in Germany.

MAKING THE FIRST CHEESE PRESS

The settlers befriended local Dominicans, but they clung to their German and Austrian roots, preferring Bach and Goethe to Caribbean music and Dominican poetry. Eventually, they built a small wooden synagogue and elementary school for their children. Sosúa became a kind of "*Heimat*" (German homeland) abroad, deeply rooted in European culture.

Meanwhile, letters from Gerda's parents and Fritz expressed worries about family members who had not escaped Germany.

Gerda worried, too. "I was always watching for our relatives' faces when Holocaust news came on Movietone News before the Saturday matinees," Gerda remembers. The Movietone News was a ten-minute newsreel featuring stories from around the world; it was played before a feature-length movie. That's where Gerda saw the headlines: "Germans beat up and murder Jews in the streets of Germany;" "Japanese bomb Pearl Harbor," and, finally, in 1941, "America enters the war."

Inspired by Fritz's success in saving the family, Gerda wanted to help her remaining classmates at her German-Jewish school. She wrote to First Lady Eleanor Roosevelt describing their dire circumstances and begged her to save her friends.

Meanwhile, Fritz was concerned about Gerda, even though she was only a teenager:

> Dear Gerda:
>
> It's important you make something of yourself at school so you can help our parents. I will do everything to keep the family healthy so you will see them again.
>
> What progress are you making in school? What are your plans?
>
> Many greetings and love. Our parents send their love, too.
>
> Your loving brother,
>
> Fritz

"I was always watching for our relatives' faces when Holocaust news came on Movietone News."

Münzenberg, im Hintergrund die Burg

Drogerie

Emil Katz

MAGG

THREE STARS IN THE NIGHT SKY

Years passed and, as the war persisted, Gerda's family remained in the Dominican Republic.

Gerda's mother wrote during Gerda's teen years: "It has been a long time since we last saw each other. You must be growing and changing, and I can't picture you now. A mother gives a part of her heart when she sends a child abroad."

Gerda wrote back, finally admitting how terribly she missed her family. Gerda's mother responded in this poignant letter:

> *Dear Gerda:*
>
> *A mother can never forget a child. Not a day goes by when I don't think of you and Adolf. Don't be sad, my little daughter. Every night, I look at three stars in the night sky and I have a little conversation. "Now, there is my dear Gerda," I say. I think of our homeland, you in Seattle, and all of us in Sosúa. Whenever I see those three beautiful, bright stars we share, I feel calmer. Look at those stars and think of me.*
>
> *All my love,*
>
> *Mutter*

After that exchange, letters between Gerda and her mother always mentioned the three stars in the night sky that mother and daughter shared.

In Seattle, when Gerda turned fourteen, she entered Garfield High School, which had a diverse population of Japanese, Chinese, black, and Jewish students. She became good friends with several Japanese-American classmates.

But in 1942, after World War II began, the government labeled Japanese-Americans — whose families had lived in the U.S. for decades — as possible spies. Government agents posted signs throughout the community that notified Japanese residents of Seattle that they must sell their homes, stores, and farms in only six days. A community that had been loyal, patriotic, productive citizens would be uprooted and

"I think of our homeland, you in Seattle, and all of us in Sosúa. Whenever I see those three beautiful, bright stars we share, I feel calmer."

Jenny Katz, Gerda's mother.

THE JAPANESE INTERNMENT

In 1942, Seattle's Japantown, a vibrant community with its own hotels, restaurants, grocers, barbershops, variety stores, and laundries, was nearly a half-century old. Located next to Garfield High School, it was only a fifteen-minute walk from the Flakses' house.

After the Japanese bombed Pearl Harbor in December 1941, military and political leaders feared Japan might attack the West Coast. Amid war hysteria, leaders became suspicious of Japanese-Americans' loyalty to the United States, fearing that these residents might be spies who could give military information to their friends and relatives in Japan. These fears were baseless; the national government knew, in fact, that Japanese-Americans were a model immigrant community.

Still, anti-Japanese rage grew and, only weeks after Pearl Harbor, in February 1942, President Roosevelt signed Executive Order 9066, relocating 127,000 people of Japanese ancestry — two-thirds of whom were American citizens — to camps in remote parts of the country. Government officials posted evacuation orders all over Japantown, giving the Japanese and Japanese-American residents only six days to sell their homes, stores, farms, and other assets.

Suddenly, Japanese doctors, lawyers, architects, real estate agents, shopkeepers — hundreds of families who had lived in the community for decades — became "enemy aliens." The government then forced most of these innocent people to leave everything behind and move to the Minidoka Center near Hunt, Idaho, or other relocation centers in remote areas of the United States. This forced incarceration of innocent people stands as one of the greatest violations of human rights in American history.

(Clockwise from left) After travelling on a special restricted train, Japanese-American internees arrive at Santa Anita Assembly Center. Last Japanese-Americans leave San Pedro, California, on a truck. Japanese-American grocery store in Oakland, California.

banished…all within one week. Gerda feared that America was becoming another Germany. The sudden and frightening uprooting of devoted citizens echoed her own experience. In Germany, it was the Jews; in America, it was the Japanese.

"There was a grocery store nearby owned by hard-working people," Gerda remembers. "They had to sell all their things for 10 cents to a dollar. One day, they were there; the next day, they were gone."

The exile is evident in Garfield High School's yearbooks: Gerda's Japanese-American classmates pictured in the 1942 *Arrow* are missing from the 1943 yearbook.

"It was devastating," she says, shaking her head. "I lost friends. They just disappeared… just as I had in Germany. It went against everything I understood about America — due process and fairness."

The executive order unsettled Gerda for another reason: Gerda also was identified as an "enemy alien" because she had come from America's other enemy — Germany.

"I wondered," she recalls, "could this happen to me?"

As Gerda navigated her politically and socially confusing teenage years alone, the Katzes continued to write weekly letters:

From Fritz in 1942:

> It must be cold in Seattle. We are sitting on a veranda and perspiring. Father has learned to ride a horse. Please send vegetable seeds.

From Fritz in 1943:

> I had malaria again for eight days. It's a tropical illness, not life threatening, but very unpleasant with terrible headaches and fever. Now I feel better.

From *Mutter* in 1943:

> We have not heard anything from Adolf. We can't give up hope!

(From left to right) Gerda's high school graduation photograph, 1944; Gerda's prom photograph, 1944; Gerda is reunited with her brother, Fritz, in 1946; one of Gerda's calendars from the 1960s; Gerda's wedding photograph, 1950; Gerda, with her first child, Jeff, in 1953; Gerda and Perry's family in 1963.

From Fritz in 1943:

> *The possibility of our getting to the United States is very difficult.*

From *Mutter* in 1944:

> *I would like to see my Gerda as a young woman. We wish you could visit. I hope you don't forget your mother language.*

From Fritz in 1945:

> *Here in the tropics, Europeans can't survive long. Every three months, we need to go somewhere in the mountains to get away from the heat.*

From Fritz in 1946:

> *Dear mother wishes to see her little Gerda again. They always call you that, even though you are no longer little.*

Gerda couldn't do much more than wait. However, whenever she met someone who might do something for her family, she asked for help. "I remember I found a man who flew little planes," she says. "I asked him if he would pick up my parents in the Dominican Republic. He said yes!"

But the man couldn't just "pick up" her family; they needed visas to leave the Dominican Republic.

In 1945 — three long years after Japanese-Americans were interned, four years after the start of a war that engulfed 110 million people and 30 nations — the United States and its allies declared victory over Nazi Germany and Japan.

Finally, now that the war was over, the Flakses were able to secure the papers necessary for Fritz to leave the Dominican Republic and join Gerda in Seattle in 1946.

Gerda adored her elder brother. "I don't know any other man like him," she says. "We'd all be dead if it weren't for Fritz."

When Gerda and Perry started having children, Gerda ached even more for her family, especially her mother.

Gerda waits and waits…

But Gerda's exile from her family did not end.

Gerda's family missed her graduation from Garfield High School in 1944. In the fall of that year, Gerda enrolled in the University of Washington and began dating a high school classmate, Perry Frumkin. After completing her freshman year, she left the university, choosing to send her tuition money to her family in the Dominican Republic.

Happily, Fritz would be able to witness Gerda and Perry's wedding on June 25, 1950, but Gerda deeply wished that her parents and her sister could have attended this joyous event. It was another milestone in Gerda's life that most members of her family would miss.

When Gerda and Perry started having children, Gerda ached even more for her family, especially her mother.

"I loved my sons and my daughter so much," she remembers. "While I was nursing my children, I always thought about my mother. I wanted my parents to know their grandchildren."

Gerda spent a lifetime waiting.

Each year, when she hung a new calendar, she believed this would be the year her parents would join her in Seattle. 1948…1949…1950...1951…1952…1953…1954…1955…1956…1957…1958…1959...

But time passed — month after month, year after year — and nothing changed.

In the Dominican Republic, the bureaucrat responsible for granting visas insisted that each family member pass a German history test before he would stamp the necessary papers to leave the country. Gerda's sister, Edith, had learning difficulties, and, year after year, she failed the test. "The bureaucrat was anti-Semitic," Gerda explains. "He wouldn't allow my family to leave, and my parents would never go without my sister. So they were stuck there."

THE KATZ FAMILY REUNITED

After decades in his entrenched position, the visa-granting bureaucrat finally retired. The new agent decided that there would be no requirement to pass a history test, and, after reviewing the family's visa application, he immediately stamped the necessary papers. In 1959, more than twenty years after Gerda had fled Germany and last seen her parents, the Katzes were free to leave the Dominican Republic. Her parents were in their seventies, and Gerda was thirty-four years old.

Finally, the day Gerda had imagined for decades arrived: She would greet her family at the Seattle-Tacoma International Airport. Fritz and she, along with their families, waited on the tarmac to see their parents walk down the steps of the PanAm flight. But when passengers got off the plane, Gerda couldn't recognize her own parents.

"*Mutter*? *Vater*?" she asked an elderly couple. These old, sickly people didn't look anything like the parents Gerda pictured from her childhood in Münzenberg.

"It was a big shock," she remembers. "Their features had changed from the hot sun and hard life in the tropics."

She hugged the strangers; they cried and moaned together. "They were so different," she remembers, "but they were my parents, and I loved them."

When they arrived in Seattle, Edith moved into Fritz's home and Gerda's parents moved into her home. They were introduced to the newest members of the family, and Gerda and her parents finally came to know each other again.

Gerda's daughter, Ann Sherman, remembers that her grandparents spoke only German, so she couldn't talk to them. "I was a little girl when they arrived," Ann explains. "They were not in good health, and my mom took care of them. My grandfather died shortly after he arrived, and my grandmother only lived another four years."

In Germany, the Nazis murdered Gerda's brother, Adolf; her grandmother, *Oma*, along with the other residents of the Jewish senior home in Bad Nauheim, and Gerda's

When the passengers got off the plane, Gerda couldn't recognize her own parents. "*Mutter? Vater?*" she asked an elderly couple.

(Left) Grandparents Jenny and Albert with their grandchild, Debbie, Fritz's daughter. Their grandchildren called them Oma *and* Opa.

THE OLD SYNAGOGUE IN MÜNZENBERG

For ninety years — 1848 to 1938 — the six Jewish families who lived in Münzenberg, including Gerda's, worshipped in the small, two-story synagogue located in the center of the city, near the Lutheran church.

But during the Nazi riot on November 10, 1938, called *Kristallnacht* (the Night of Broken Glass), Nazis smashed the synagogue's door and threw benches and Jewish artifacts out the building's windows. On the street in front of the synagogue, Nazis burned the benches and the treasured Torah scrolls. However, Nazis didn't burn down the building, fearing that neighboring houses could catch fire.

After *Kristallnacht*, German Jewish families became convinced that their lives were in danger. In Münzenberg, two Jewish families were able to flee the country, but the others didn't have a place to go or they couldn't get the necessary papers to leave. Eventually, they were sent to concentration camps where Nazis murdered members of those Münzenberg families.

In 1952, the city of Münzenberg bought the old synagogue and converted it into a fire station. Workers removed the round arched windows that identified the building as a synagogue and installed a garage door and a false concrete ceiling. The building served the fire brigade until 2005, when the station moved to a new location. Then, the community debated what to do with the old building.

Before World War II, 2,800 synagogues dotted Germany; now, only 130 remain. In the last few decades, Germans have had a renewed interest in the Jewish history of their country, and they have restored many of the synagogues that survived *Kristallnacht*.

After much debate, the city council decided to spend 475,000 euros of public and private money to restore the exterior of the old synagogue to its original state. In 2009, the building was reopened as a living monument to the Jews who once lived in the city and as a cultural center for the current residents of Münzenberg.

classmates who wrote in her *Poesiealbum* — including Friedel. Only one other Jewish family of the six who lived in Gerda's German town survived. The town didn't know what to do with the Jewish synagogue that was built in 1848; it was a reproachful monument to a painful chapter in the community's history. A lumberyard was built on top of the Jewish cemetery, erasing the memory of the Jews who lived in Münzenberg for 1,000 years.

Today, most Jewish refugees have left the Dominican Republic; about twenty-five families remain on the island, and they did intermarry, as dictator Rafael Trujillo had hoped. The dairy business the Jews of Sosúa built supplies most of the butter and cheese consumed in the country today, and a few of the town's streets bear the names of its prominent Jewish residents: Dr. Rosen Street and David Stern Street. The town's synagogue and a museum remain. The final caption of the museum's exhibit reads: "Sosúa, a community born of pain and nurtured in love, must in the final analysis, represent the ultimate triumph of life."

In the 1970s, Jewish refugees organized a reunion of the former residents of the Dominican Republic. Fritz flew from Seattle to the island country for the first time in decades. The pilot learned of some of his unusual passengers. When the flight was about to land in the Dominican Republic, the pilot spoke to the passengers on the intercom, telling the other travelers the story of the brutal dictator who offered Jewish refugees a place to live when most countries around the world slammed their doors.

"To those passengers attending the reunion in Sosúa," the pilot said, with a catch in his voice, "welcome home!"

In 2011, when Gerda was eighty-six years old, compassionate students changed her life in an incredible turn of events. Eighth-graders from Madison Junior High School in Naperville, Illinois, read the historical novel, *Is It Night or Day?,* which introduced them to the two terrified twelve-year-olds, Gerda and Edith, who met on the ship and forged a deep bond during the rough ten-day passage in March of 1938. Gerda was seasick and Edith took care of her, refusing to leave her side. But sadly, when the two friends parted in New York City, they lost touch with each other. For decades, Edith yearned to see Gerda again.

Moved by Edith and Gerda's story of friendship, the students made it a class project to locate and reunite the two who hadn't seen each other in seventy-three years. With only Gerda's maiden name, the name of the ship, and Gerda's destination, the eighth-graders combed through hundreds of online sources.

The real breakthrough came when the students found Gerda's wedding announcement, which gave them her married name. Eventually, the students found an article in a 2010 local newsletter announcing Gerda and her husband's sixtieth anniversary. When the students read in the article that Gerda Frumkin had fled Nazi Germany, they knew they had found Edith's childhood immigration friend.

The first time Gerda and Edith talked on the phone in 2011, just a few weeks before they would meet in person, they said hello and then, for twenty minutes, they sobbed together. No words were necessary. Each felt the other was the only person who understood their deep uprooting and unbearable losses.

Gerda Katz Frumkin and Edith Westerfeld Schumer.

During their dramatic reunion in Seattle, Edith told Gerda, "I wish we could have been in touch. I think we could have helped each other."

"At evening-tide she climbed up into a little tree, and purposed spending the night there, for fear of the wild beasts." Illustration by Warwick Goble for "The Fairy Book."

During their dramatic reunion in Seattle, Edith told Gerda, "I wish we could have been in touch. I think we could have helped each other."

At that time, the two resumed their friendship, sometimes talking on the phone twice a week. Gerda had never spoken of her traumatic childhood. Edith encouraged Gerda to tell her story to her friends, children, and grandchildren. Gerda gave Edith unconditional love and understanding.

Before they would end their phone conversations, the two old friends had a ritual.

Edith would tell Gerda, "You are my sister."

And Gerda would whisper into the receiver, "And you are my sister."

The two spoke in German and English. They giggled like schoolgirls. They shared the ups and downs of their lives. They fretted about politics and world affairs. They cried together about the weight of their shared history.

Looking back, Gerda sees how her childhood immigration and losses defined her. She could have written her own Grimms' fairy tale.

Most of all, they stepped into each other's lives and filled in some of the holes.

Looking back, Gerda sees how her childhood immigration and losses defined her. "I was so upset by these experiences, I never left my husband's side, not even for one night," she explains. "I never left the U.S. I lived in the same house for fifty-five years. I was afraid to leave home."

Gerda Katz from Münzenberg could have written her own Grimms' fairy tale, like "Rapunzel," "The Pied Piper of Hamelin," or "Cinderella."

Except her story is not folklore; it is all painfully true.

IN MEMORIAM: GERDA KATZ FRUMKIN
DECEMBER 4, 1925 – SEPTEMBER 22, 2017

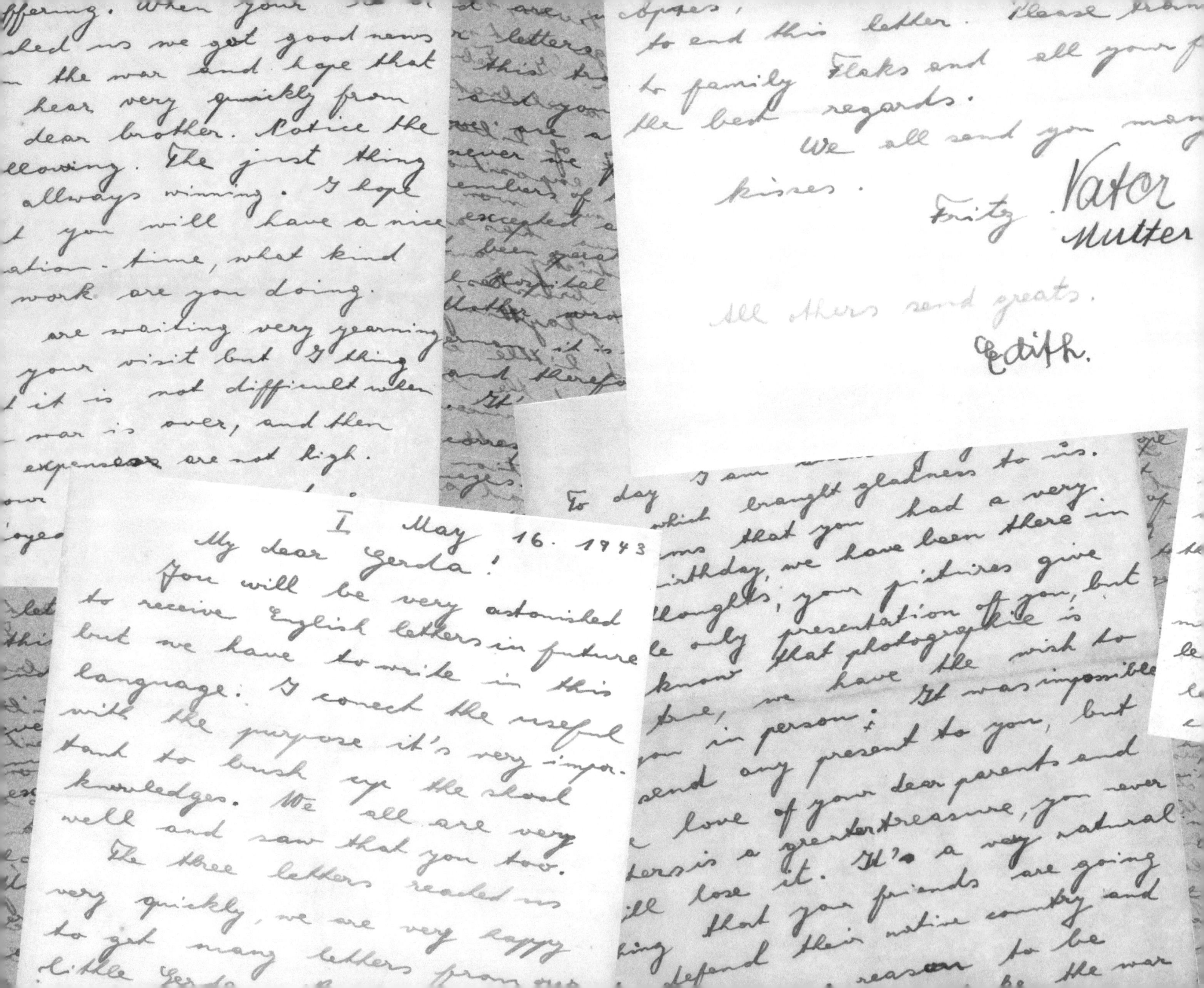

...ffering. When your ...
...ded us we got good news ...
...n the war and hope that
...hear very quickly from
...dear brother. Notice the
...eaving. The first thing
...allways winning. I hope
...t you will have a nice
...ation-time, what kind
work are you doing.

...are waiting very yearning
...your visit but I thing
...it is not difficult when
...war is over, and then
...expenses are not high.

...to end this letter. Please ...
...to family Fleks and all your ...
...the best regards.

We all send you man...
kisses.

Fritz. **Vater**
Mutter

All others send greats.

Edith.

I   May   16. 1943
My dear Gerda!
You will be very astonished
to receive English letters in future
but we have to write in this
language. I coach the useful
with the purpose it's very important to brush up the school
knowledges. We all are very
well and saw that you too.
The three letters reached us
very quickly, we are very happy
to get many letters from ...
little Gerda ...

To day I am ...
...which brought gladness to us.
...ms that you had a very
...irthday, we have been there in
...houghts, your pictures give
...e only presentation of you, but
...know that photographie is
...true, we have the wish to
...you in person: It was impossible
...send any present to you, but
...love of your dear parents and
...ters is a greater treasure, you never
...will lose it. It's a very natural
...ting that your friends are going
...defend their native country and
...reason to be
...the war

[Overlapping handwritten letter fragments]

Top-left fragment:

...and send you the best wishes a
...heartiest congratulations and hope
...that we have the favour to see
... in the next year. You wrote
...at you are saving money to
...it is, we invite you and family
...ks and surely hope that you will
...e. Dear Mother wishes to
...her little Gerda. They always
...so, you know the story
...Kochs foal (colt) it had an
...twenty years and they called
...allway foal, dear mother does
...same. Your pictures look
...nice we see that you are in
...st lands and are so glad for it.
...you have to learn very
... in preparation of
...examine

Top-center/right fragment:

I bought
for dear mother and aunt
Bertha, and now I beg you
to send some pattern very soon.
We need a shirt, a pair of
drawers (short all for tropical use)
and an undervest, the last is
for men they carry it under the
shirt, bu... pattern. In
one of th...
or new, ... a long time, for I know
day ... our letters ... and you need it. your last
regards to ...and all your letter arrived very quickly,
...the time of five days we
...very enjoyed with the nice

Right fragment:

7th Sept.
My dear Gerda!
I don't like to let wait
a long time, for I know
our letters are parts of your
and you need it. Your last
letter arrived very quickly,
the time of five days we
very enjoyed with the nice
in shortness you get some fro...
days separate us fro...
...we have the be...
...d wishes for you
...hoped that we
...of our dear bro...
ill be the happiest
life. With my
...ledges you make
...ments, I know

Bottom fragment:

August 28th 1943

My dear Gerda!
To day you get the answer of your last letter
from July 11th! I was very glad to receive your
best birthday-wishes, every year I have the hope
to be together with you for there is a better chance
to use all my knowledges but our principal wish
is that our dear brother Adolf will soon be delivered
Can you correct my letters, it's very important
for me. I think that the expression of my style
...right I should be glad to learn more English

Gerda Katz Frumkin and the author in 2015.

Fern Schumer Chapman is the author of several award-winning books:
Motherland: A Mother/Daughter Journey to Reclaim the Past; Is It Night or Day?; Middle School Sleuths: How an Eighth-Grade Class Reunited Two Holocaust Refugees; and *Facing the Past: A Public Memorial Art Compels a Small German Town to Confront Its History*. A sought-after speaker, she has presented to schools, libraries, charity events and women's organizations. She lives in northern Illinois.

www.fernschumerchapman.com

PHOTO CREDITS

Cover - Photograph by Gilles Tarabiscuite

Endpages - letters from Fritz and others - Courtesy of Gerda Katz

Photo of children fleeing - http://www.ushmm.org/

Photo of children in Syrian refugee camp - CNS photo/Sedat Suna, EPA

Photo of Gerda as child - Gerda Katz personal collection

Illustration of Snow White - Franz Jüttner, https://commons.wikimedia.org

Photo of Castle Münzenberg - http://view.stern.de/de/mitglieder/Quasimodo1976

Photo of Gerda's family - Gerda Katz personal collection

Photo of Gerda with her pet chicken - Gerda Katz personal collection

Photo of Storm Troopers at Castle Münzenberg in 1931 - Philipp Pfaff, Butzbach, www.lagis-hessen.de

Photo of burning in front of west tower at Castle Münzenberg in 1931 - Philipp Pfaff, Butzbach, www.lagis-hessen.de

Two photos of Nazi propaganda:

    1932 election poster - https://medium.com/@HolocaustMuseum/

    1938 poster "All the people say 'Yes.'" - https://www.pinterest.com/

Photo of Storm Troopers - http://spartacus-educational.com/GERsa.htm

Headshot of Kurt Mayer - https://www.plu.edu/resolute/spring-2015/germany-jterm/

Postcard of the Jewish School in Bad Nauheim - https://www.plu.edu/resolute/spring-2015/germany-jterm/

Photo of burning of synagogue items in Mosbach - http://somewereneighbors.ushmm.org/

Photo of Gerda's passport - Gerda Katz personal collection

Photo of Jenny and Fritz Katz - Gerda Katz personal collection

Photo of five friends on bicycle - Gerda Katz personal collection

Posiealbum - Gerda Katz personal collection

Photo of children looking out porthole - gettyimages.com

Photo of Gerda Katz - Gerda Katz personal collection

Photograph of Seattle 1931 - Seattle Times archive

Gerda's Alien Registration card - Gerda Katz personal collection

Photo of Gerda's foster parents - Gerda Katz personal collection

Photo of the Flak's boarding house - Fern Schumer Chapman personal collection

Letters from family – Gerda Katz personal collection

Fritz Katz - Gerda Katz personal collection

Photo of refugees in the Dominican Republic - http://archives.jdc.org/project/dominican-republic-dorsa/

Newspaper clip - The New York Times

Photo of family at Dominican Republic homestead - Gerda Katz personal collection

Photo of Nazis rounding up Jews 1944 - Bundesarchiv, Bild 101I-680-8285A-26 / Faupel / CC-BY-SA 3.0

Photo of Rafael Trujillo - http://sosuafilm.com/about/history.html

Postcard of Evian, France - Fern Schumer Chapman personal collection

Photo of Signing of Agreement - http://blog.nli.org.il/en/tropical_zion/

Photo of Fritz with Horses - Gerda Katz personal collection

Photo of the Settlement - http://images.archives.jdc.org/

Photo of the Synagogue - http://blog.nli.org.il/en/tropical_zion/

Photo of Fritz on the tractor - Gerda Katz personal collection

Photo of Albert, Edith, and Jenny - Gerda Katz personal collection

Photo of Milking Cow - http://blog.nli.org.il/en/tropical_zion/

Photo of Making the first Cheese Press - http://images.archives.jdc.org/

Photo of Gerda on bench - Gerda Katz personal collection

Photo of MovieTone News - http://library.sc.edu/p/collections/mirc

Photo of Gerda - Gerda Katz personal collection

Photo of family in Dominican Republic - Gerda Katz personal collection

Postcard from Münzenberg - Gerda Katz personal collection

Photo of family in front of Münzenberg pharmacy - Gerda Katz personal collection

Photo of Night Sky - Jason Jennings/cosmicphotos.com

Photo of Jenny Katz - Gerda Katz personal collection

Photo of "I Am American" - Dorothea Lange/Courtesy National Archives and Records Administration

Photo of Japanese on truck with wooden slats - Clem Albers/Courtesy National Archives and Records Administration

Photo of Japanese arriving at Santa Anita Assembly Center - Clem Albers/Courtesy National Archives and Records Administration

All photos on pages 34 and 35 - Gerda Katz personal collection; calendar - Gerda Katz personal collection

Photo of Gerda Katz - Gerda Katz personal collection

Photo of Albert and Jenny Katz - Gerda Katz personal collection

Photo of Jenny Katz and Ann Sherman - Gerda Katz personal collection

Photo of Jenny and Albert Katz with grandchild - Gerda Katz personal collection

Photo of Münzenberg synagogue - Gert Krell provided these photos from the Mayor's office in Münzenberg

Photo of Gerda Katz and Edith Westerfeld Schumer - Fern Schumer Chapman personal collection

Fairytale illustration by Warwick Goble - https://www.pinterest.co.uk/pin/340373684316258865/

Photo of Gerda Katz in front of water - Gerda Katz personal collection

ACKNOWLEDGEMENTS

I couldn't have created this book without the images Lyn Frumkin provided from Gerda's personal archive of photographs. He spent hours and hours organizing hundreds of images, many of which appear in this book.

Thank you, Garfield High School Career and Technology Education Instructor Corey E. Louviere and junior Aiden Kemper, for providing the old *Arrow* yearbooks from 1941-1943. Those photographs helped me to understand how the Japanese internment affected Gerda and her classmates. Thanks to my friend, Gert Krell, for tracking down the historical images of the Münzenberg synagogue.

I am indebted to the fine work of my editorial and design team, Tom Greensfelder, Bruce Wasser, and Susan Figliulo. Each makes a unique contribution and, together, we bring my stories to life on the page.

A special thanks to Junior Library Guild Editorial Director Susan Marston and my friends at JLG, who continue to support my work.

Finally, thanks to my mother, Edith Westerfeld Schumer, who has been my inspiration and my travel companion on this incredible journey that led us to Gerda Katz.

THE LEGACY OF THE HOLOCAUST
AWARD-WINNING THREE-BOOK SERIES

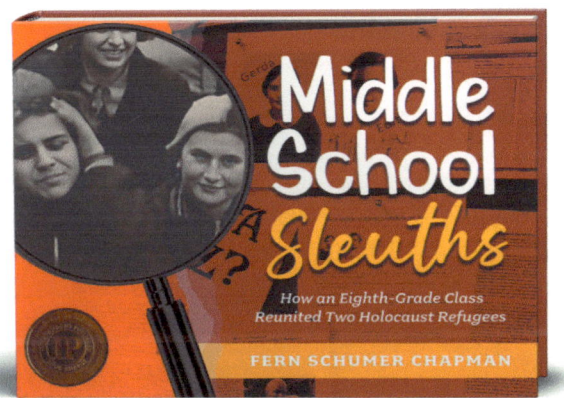

Book 1: **Middle School Sleuths** - A nonfiction work that captures how an 8th-grade class reunited two Holocaust refugees 73 years after they had immigrated together. Featured by Oprah.

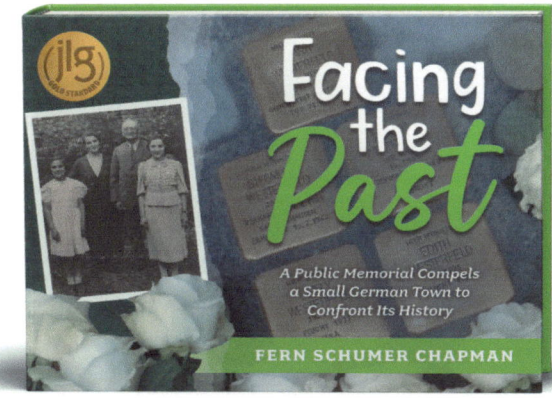

Book 2: **Facing the Past** - A story of atonement - witness the 2014 installation of memorial stones for one family, as Stockstadt residents face their Holocaust history.

Book 3: **Three Stars in the Night Sky** - How one Jewish family escaped Nazi Germany through a little-known program. Their story reflects the dislocating trauma of the immigrant experience.